A gift for:

From:

WRITTEN BY STUART & LINDA MACFARLANE
EDITED BY HELEN EXLEY
ILLUSTRATIONS BY ROLAND FIDDY & JULIETTE CLARKE

Published in 2019 by Helen Exley® LONDON in Great Britain.
Illustrations by Roland Fiddy and Juliette Clarke © Helen Exley Creative Ltd 2019.
All the words by Stuart & Linda Macfarlane © Helen Exley Creative Ltd 2019.
Design, selection and arrangement are all © Helen Exley Creative Ltd 2019.

ISBN: 978-1-78485-238-2

12 11 10 9 8 7 6 5 4 3 2 1

OTHER HELEN EXLEY GIFTBOOKS:

For my beautiful Granddaughter 365

The Resilience Book

Inspiration 365

365 Simpler Days

The book of Positive Thoughts

Yes to life! 365

The Secrets of Happiness 365

The little book of Gratitude

Over 70's Jokes

Helen Exley® LONDON, 16 Chalk Hill, Watford, Herts WD19 4BG, UK
www.helenexley.com

January 1

This was a real
Red Letter day for me –
a day to be remembered
and cherished forever.
I wonder
what happened!

WHAT IS A HELEN EXLEY GIFTBOOK?

We hope you enjoy *Senior Moments*. It's just one of many hilarious cartoon publications available from Helen Exley®LONDON, all of which make special gifts. We try our best to bring you the funniest jokes because we want every book we publish to be great to give, great to receive.

Helen Exley®LONDON creates gifts for all special occasions – not just birthdays, anniversaries and weddings, but for those times when you just want to say 'thanks' or make someone laugh. Why not visit our website ***www.helenexley.com*** and browse through all our gift ideas.

January 2

"Knock Knock"
"Who's there?"
"I don't know."
"Oh dear...
neither do I."

December 31

End of Year
Celebration:
Little old me!
Yippeeeee!!!!
I have survived
another year.

January 3

Sometimes it's useful to appear
to be having a senior moment —
such as when "forgetfully" eating
another doughnut.

December 30

I always find the last days of the year
very nostalgic. It's an emotionally
charged time, a time for reflection,
for quiet contemplation.
I can't help but look back
on the year that has passed
and wonder
what on earth happened.

The secret to longevity
is to look death
in the eye and say
"I'll be along shortly,"
then forget
what you said.

December 29

My best friend went to a presentation, "Ten Methods to Achieve a Perfect Memory". He taught my wife all five techniques and she taught them to me. So here are all the ways to achieve a perfect memory, Uhh… uh… where do I start!

January 5

I haven't lost
my youthful agility –
I just don't remember
where I put it.

Senior moments!

At 82 I'm not as strong as I was when I was 22, I am not as fit as I was when I was 22 and I'm definitely not as good looking as I was when I was 22. But I have one characteristic that all the 80 year old ladies adore – I've forgotten…

The police didn't believe me when I explained that I was driving fast so that I could reach my destination before I forgot where I was going.

Today I feel like
a computer
that's been downgraded
from a
Duel Core 2.4 GHz
Processor
to an abacus.

January 7

I can't remember the last time
I forgot something.

When I woke this morning
I thought I'd died
and gone to Heaven.
Turned out it was not an angel –
just my wife
in her new white night dress.

Life is like a bottle of
Champagne:
full of fizz, razzmatazz
and celebration.
It's rather sad that,
when you are so old,
you become incapable
of getting the cork out.

December 25

Senior moments!

I love everything about my gifts – the flowers, too much to eat, getting another twenty-two handkerchiefs... and, of course, one can never have too many pairs of novelty socks!

January 9

Knock Knock.
Who's there?
I am.
I am who?
Now you're getting me confused.

December 24

Now that I'm retired
I feel obliged
to take up knitting and make
everyone garish sweaters
that are far too big.

Senior moments!

My daughter bought me a parrot
to keep me company.
I've tried very hard to teach it
to talk but the silly thing can only
say three phrases:
* I don't remember that.
* Where are the car keys?
*Oh my knees hurt.

I discovered today that,
after the age of twelve,
it becomes unacceptable
to repeatedly
knock on doors and run away.
I must admit
the police were
very understanding.

January 11

Reaching the age
of eighty
is like winning
the lottery
only to discover
that you have lost
the ticket.

My special comb –
the one that has served me
well for over forty years
has now no purpose.
It idles in my
dressing table drawer
alongside my hopes
and aspirations.

January 12

I have a strict morning routine.
Before I get out of bed I do a full
inventory of all my ailments:
Do my knees hurt? Is my gout painful?
Does my back ache? And so on.
After assessing everything,
if I have got at least three "yeses"
I can be reasonably sure
that I am still alive.

The Irony of Old Age:

* You can afford to do all the things you are no longer capable of doing.

* You have years of experience but no one wants to know.

* You have an abundance of nose and ear hair but none on your head.

* You know everything but can recall nothing.

January 13

I have learned from decades of experience that things go in and out of fashion in regular cycles. Because of that I keep absolutely everything so as to save money. It has worked well with all my clothes and jewellery. I'm just hoping that typewriters and black-and-white cameras make a comeback sometime soon.

Senior moments!

Age has not stopped me
from doing the things I want.
No, it's being unfit,
overweight
and lethargic
that's done that.

January 14

I have developed
an amazing technique
that enables me
to recall things –
I ask my wife.

My ability to do algebra, trigonometry and calculus
hasn't changed at all over the decades.
In my declining years they are still the mystery
they were when I was a teenager.

January 15

I hate it when I'm in town and I feed all my change
into the roadside parking meter –
only to discover that I travelled there by bus.
It's such a nuisance having to go all the way home
for the car and hoping the space is still available
when I get back.

If there were no mirrors
in the world
would my face still be wrinkly?

January 16

I wish every day was my birthday...
that way I wouldn't have to try to remember
which date it's on.

December 17

My wife and I have been together for so long we can read each other's minds. I know hers is full of fuzzy thoughts and she knows mine is completely blank.

January 17

Last night my partner
and I had a night of wild,
unadulterated passion –
we played
Scrabble until two
in the morning.

December 16

When watching television
I often need to get my wife
to remind me of the plot...
those children's shows
can get pretty complicated.

My dating site age: 59
My legal age: 73
The age I feel: 94
The age I act: 11

Most of the time
I have no idea
which day of the week it is
until I take
my day-coded pills.

January 19

Eat vitamin pills, exercise regularly,
forget just as often.

December 14

I've reached the age when even my imaginary friends are having hip replacements and heart surgery.

January 20

I often wish
that I could live my life
backward – that way
I could forget things
before they happened.

Car problems again today.
On the fifty mile journey it wouldn't go above
five miles per hour. Eventually, in great frustration,
I took it to the local garage.
Apparently it's the same problem I've had
a number of times – the technical term
that the mechanic used was
You-Have-Left-The-Handbrake-On-Again.

January 21

I often get the two mixed up –
my age and my cell phone number.

December 12

I have just finished writing
my autobiography.
I tried getting it published
but it seems there is
little demand for books
that are less
than fifty pages long.

January 22

I eat healthy foods
that help feed my brain;
blueberries, salmon and eggs.
Recently I very nearly
ate some broccoli!

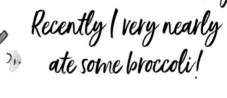

December 11

Dear Diary:

I had a serious senior moment today.
Coming out of the cinema I forgot
I'd gone by car and so took
the train home. I'd gone about five miles
before the train driver managed
to wrestle the controls from me.

Senior moments!

I took a trip down memory lane
and got totally lost.

December 10

I used to thoroughly hate Monday
because it was the first day
of the working week.
Now I am free to hate any day
of the week
quite indiscriminately.

January 24

Some face the prospect
of getting older with
sadness and melancholy.
That's not my way –
I prefer wailing
and weeping.

December 9

The older you get
the less sleep you get,
the less sleep you get
the older
you appear.

I am not that old –
I am just a little past my sell-by date.

Senior moments!

Dear Diary:

Today I feel a total idiot
as I sat at the piano trying to play
Frédéric François Chopin's
Piano Concerto No. 1 in E Minor.
No matter how hard I tried
I kept hitting the wrong notes.
It wasn't until later that I realised –
I have never played
the piano before.

Be positive today
for tomorrow is going to be worse.

Every morning and every evening
I do fifty push-ups.
Then I sleep in a desperate effort
to build my energy reserves back up

January 27

Senior moments!

For years I regularly got into trouble for forgetting to get my wife a birthday gift, our anniversary or other significant events. I've solved that problem. I have arranged with the florist to deliver a bouquet of flowers every single day with a card that says, "Delete as required: Happy Birthday / Happy Anniversary / Happy Special Day / Have a Nice Day."

December 6

That internet thing is useless!
I tried it. I asked it
where I had put my car keys -
it hadn't a clue.

January 28

I have a really great game
that I love to play
with my grandchildren.
They go and find
a good hiding place
while I count to ten
then forget
to search for them.

My memory has a mind
of its own – sometimes
I can remember things
I haven't even forgotten
and forget things
I haven't even remembered.

I forgot my zimmer frame
when I set out for the local shop
this morning. Truth is
I don't really need it –
it wasn't until I fell
for the fourth time
that I realised I'd
gone out without it.

December 4

I've been given so many
spare body parts that I've just been presented
with an award for recycling.

Senior moments!

I hate when it happens and it's happening more frequently – my husband and I meet someone I know from the past and, to be polite, I have to make the introductions. And I'm thinking at top speed and the name is on the tip of my tongue but I can't quite remember it. So the best I can do is blurt out, "And this is my husband, Thingy."

December 3

Senior moments!

After thirty years
I am back in the dating game.
However I have a real dilemma –
on a first date
do you snog with your teeth in
or your teeth out?

I find that with age I am becoming more indecisive. Last night while playing chess I couldn't decide between the Queen's Gambit and the Ruy Lopez openings. Eventually I thought, "What the heck" and got my little horse to jump over the soldier thing and just got on with the game.

Life:
your catheter bag
will burst while
you are trying
on clothes in
an expensive shop!

My granddaughter
seemed rather impressed
when I told her that I'd
downloaded a movie
for us to watch.
But she was rather confused
when I told her
that it had been up
in the attic for years.

Senior moments!

I hate flying but recently I had no option but to take a long distance flight. I boarded the plane, found my seat and braced myself for the horrors ahead.

I was relieved when the plane eventually came to a halt. Keen to get off I sprang to my feet – only to be reprimanded by the flight attendant. Apparently we had just done something called "taxiing to the runway".

Dear Diary:

I am at Everest Base Camp.
I must have taken the wrong turning
on the way to the supermarket.

The flight to New York went very smoothly though goodness knows how I got here without my passport or tickets. I guess I'd better phone my wife and let her know where I am.

Why is it that my mind thinks
I'm fourteen,
my legs think I'm
ninety-four
but I'm actually
seventy-four?

Senior moments!

Dear Diary:
I went to the doctor's
for a check-up today.
He says that as I'm more than
50% spare parts
he's going to have to refer me
to the local garage!

February 4

I read that carrots
are supposed to improve
your memory.
Nonsense!
I ate twelve yesterday
but the car keys
are still missing!

November 28

Senior moments!

If you can't find
your spectacles anywhere
there is an 87% chance
that you are actually
wearing them.

February 5

I used to hate all the spam phone calls
I received but now I amuse myself
by making up stories to keep
the caller on the line.
Recently I told one scammer
that I'd won the lottery
and was giving half of the money
to the first person to call me.
I got twenty minutes of fun
out of that one.

Senior moments!

Your new television will not come with
an instruction manual because it's so simple
it can be operated by an eight year old –
unfortunately you don't have an eight year old
to show you how to work it.

Senior moments!

I went on an
orientation course
last week –
now I can find my way
from the bedroom
to the kitchen...
most of the time.

My husband
got very upset because
I forgot his birthday.
Truth is I didn't forget
his birthday –
I forgot
I was married!

Justin laughs uncontrollably as he watches
the two muscled young lads surf in from the sea on
a huge wave, run across the beach
then zoom off in an expensive sports car
with their beautiful girlfriends.
Justin laughs, "Sorry but as I watched those lads
I couldn't help but think that before too long
they will be as old and wrinkly as I am."

At my age the medicine
one takes for one ailment
cancels out the benefit
of the medicine taken
for another ailment.

February 8

Senior moments!

A t the age of ninety-five I married
a man thirty years younger than me.
To be honest I had a long and thorough
debate with myself as to whether
marrying someone so much younger
was a sensible idea.
I was torn in two directions:
My head said, "No" but my pacemaker
said, "Yes! Yes! Yes!"

Senior moments!

My best friend
never remembers birthdays –
that's why she thinks
she's still forty-nine.

February 9

I forget something new every day.

I forgot to take
my Viagra before going
to bed last night.
Probably just as well –
it's another seven months
before I get my
birthday treat.

February 10

Senior moments!

My friends and I still love to play Scrabble even though we are now all over eighty. We haven't lost our touch and can come up with some very interesting words. I wish I could remember one!

Senior moments!

Dear Diary:

I have a nagging feeling that today
is the birthday of a friend or relation.
I do hope it's not someone I should
have bought a gift for. Hold on!
What if it's my birthday and everyone
else has forgotten!!

I must say that I have accepted
my age with grace and dignity.
Apart from the hair implants,
the face lift and the tummy tuck
I have happily embraced
nature's cruel folly.

To accommodate my bad memory
I have spreadsheets for absolutely everything.
I have spreadsheets to keep track of my finances,
my clothes, my travel, stamp collection,
birthdays and anniversaries.
I am so dependent on my spreadsheets
to manage my life that I have
now got a master spreadsheet
to track all my other spreadsheets.

February 12

Old age is an opportunity
to do all those crazy things
your mother wouldn't let you do
as a child.

November 20

*I never lie about my age...
well, truth is, I can never remember my age.*

My grandson was raving about
his new virtual reality headset
and trying very hard
to get me to try it.
I declined.
Right now I'm having
enough trouble
understanding normal reality
without experiencing
some virtual one.

November 19

I am a party
animal –
think sloth
with a
pink balloon.

February 14

Dear Diary:

I am very disappointed for
I did not receive a single
Valentine card today.
Which is very surprising
for I am sure
that I sent myself two.

My wife and I love television quiz shows.
Sometimes, between us we can answer
three or four correctly –
provided we use the "pause" button
to give us extra thinking time.

I forgot to get my wife
a Valentine card this year.
It's fortunate for me
that she received four cards
and two huge bouquets
anonymously.
That was a lucky escape!

I have had so many
body parts replaced
my wife has taken to calling me
her million dollar man.

February 16

If you have looked
absolutely everywhere
it must be in your
underwear drawer.

I've a photographic memory –
sadly it's all
in black and white
and a bit fuzzy.

February 17

I've reached the age
when I've heard it all,
seen it all
and done it all.
It's just a great pity
that I've also
forgotten it all.

I have reached the point
where it is no longer
appropriate for me to say,
"I got such a fright
I had a heart attack."
Whenever I do this my partner
dashes for the phone to call
emergency services.

February 18

I thought I'd give walking football a try. I had scored twenty goals before I was asked to leave the pitch. They didn't like my high powered mobility scooter when playing.

When I can't remember
someone's name,
I think I just say
something like,
"Is your health problem
any better?"

Senior moments!

It's hard to
impress people
with your body's
disasters
when you can't
remember the list!

Senior moments!

I discovered today
that it is not a good idea
to get my mobility scooter
washed in one of those
automated car washes.
I got thoroughly soaked.

February 20

Senior moments!

It was a good idea to get
"*Left*" and "*Right*"
tattooed on my hands...
but I deeply regret getting
Old Joe to do the job.
I can't remember if he got it right.

Just like Hercule Poirot
I like to keep my brain cells active.
Seven or eight times every day
I give them a challenging puzzle
to solve –
"Where have I put my
dentures now?"

February 21

I go to bed at 7pm every night.
That's like 2am in teenage-time.

Oh, the bitter sweet irony of it all. As a youngster I desperately wanted a really fast sports car but could never afford one. Now I regularly get to dash across town in a high speed ambulance.

February 22

I'm too old to be sensible and too sensible to be old.

My Keep Young and Beautiful Mantra:
I am not getting old.
My face is not wrinkled like a rhino.
That twinge is definitely not rheumatism.
My knees work perfectly –
most of the time.
Ouch, ooh, eech, oh ah, ouch...

I got a shock this morning –
I seriously thought I was dead.
I was staring at my watch in disbelief,
it read 8:42 and it refused to change!
Then I realised it was
the battery that was dead –
not me.

zzZZZ

Life:
your brand new spectacles
are never as good
as the tatty old pair
they replaced.

My grandchildren were giggling and laughing with delight for they thought I was doing an impersonation of a frog. Sadly I now make that croaking sound every time I kneel down or get up again.

Today I made a very bold decision.
I have decided to stop fixating
on the many, many, many things
that I can no longer do.
Instead I will focus on the positive
and concentrate my energy
on the thing that I can still do
brilliantly – moan!

February 25

I have eight pairs
of spectacles –
that way I randomly
lose one pair at about
the same rate as
I randomly find another.

Senior moments!

All the youngsters are so keen on keeping fit.
We didn't have time in our days to go running around
the streets half-naked in expensive sporty clothes.
When we were young we got all the exercise
we needed by playing games of
"Knock the Door and Run Away".

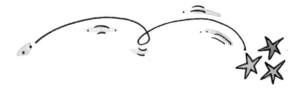

Dear Diary:

I seem to have gotten into
the habit of repeating
everything twice.
I seem to have gotten
into the habit of
repeating everything
twice.

My brother asked
what I'd like
for my 80th birthday.
"To be 40,"
I replied.

For the last six months I have been regularly
buying an expensive rejuvenation cream
on an internet site. It claims that it will
make you feel like a teenager again.
In a way it worked – after buying it for six months
I feel as poor as I did when I was a student.

Senior moments!

I downloaded a fantastic App
to help me remember things.
Every twenty minutes
it sends me a reminder
that I downloaded
a fantastic App to help me
remember things.

It is not until
I've climbed into bed that I remember
that I need to switch the light off first.

Senior moments!

I have got old age sorted. When sent to the supermarket I came back with a goldfish. When asked to wash the dishes I "accidentally" broke the best crockery and when told to do the ironing I burnt my wife's best blouse. I have now been banned from doing all household chores.

March 1

Dear Diary:

Today I did a parachute jump from
an aeroplane. It was a great surprise
to my daughter who was watching
from the ground for she thought
I was flying off to Bermuda.
I really must try to be less cantankerous
with cabin crew next time.

November 3

Senior moments!

If you can't do
at least one
outrageous thing
before breakfast
you are wasting
your old age.

Baldness:

On the upside I don't have to wash my hair.
On the downside it takes me twice as long
to wash my face.

Senior moments!

We met a lovely couple
while we were away.
I must confess that I now feel
rather guilty that I told them
that I am forty-nine...
especially as my son
had just admitted
to being fifty-two.

I had a very difficult upbringing.
My family of twelve lived
in a cold dank cave with just fragments
of animal skin to protect us from
the freezing snows.
If my father didn't manage to catch
a sabre tooth tiger we could be hungry
for many days... Sorry, that's ridiculous –
it was lions we ate.

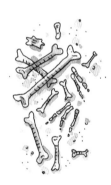

Senior moments!

I am still up for wild adventures. This morning
I gave some serious thought to doing
a 100 mile wild swim. Tomorrow I plan to give some
serious thought to climbing both Mount Kilimanjaro
and Mount Everest.
This thinking about adventure is exhausting –
so soon I will take a few days off to rest.

I have one of those cars
that you don't need to drive
because it operates
using a what-do-you-call-
it... ah, yes, a husband.

I was awoken by a knock at the door...
"Thump... thump... thump."
Unwillingly I struggled from my sofa and,
with chilled heart, slowly crossed the room.
Opening the door I saw there against
a dark sky the unmistakable vision
of The Grim Reaper.
And in that bleak moment
I knew that the dreaded day
had at last arrived... it was Hallowe'en.

March 5

Senior moments!

An active mind is a healthy mind –
that's my philosophy. I keep my mind active
by doing my jigsaw puzzle every day – I've very
nearly finished the one from six months ago
and looking forward to starting another
sometime soon.

I won't have to buy
a mask this Halloween –
my wrinkled face
sends shivers of horror
down the spine
of everyone I meet.

Senior moments!

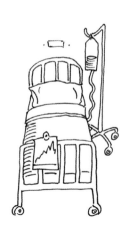

I've spent so much
of this year
in hospital that they
have invited me
to their staff party.

"Don't worry. Be happy."
Yeah right!
What makes me happiest is being
thoroughly miserable and making
everyone else feel miserable
with my apocalyptic predictions
of the terrible things
that are about to happen.

Boring Event:
when you get that
fabulous new jumper
home you discover
it's the same as
the one you bought
last week.

Senior moments!

I may not have much choice
    but to grow old
but I will never, ever,
    ever grow up –
my doll collection now
totals over five hundred.

Senior moments!

I am eighty-five but feel like
a twenty year old –
well to be more precise I feel like
a twenty year old
who has rheumatics, gout,
a dodgy hip and
has the facial complexion
of an aged elephant.

I went to the football stadium today. I must say I found it very boring sitting there for hours. My wife says I should try going back when there is a match on.

Senior moments!

My son bought me one of those
new-fangled GPS watches
for my birthday –
not a lot of use to me,
I am still trying to get the hang
of the sundial.

Age is only a number –
a very, very big and frightening number.

....88, 89, 90, 91, 92, 93, 94,

95, 96, 97, 98, 99, 100, 101 ......

I had my annual medical
examination today.
My doctor says that I am
normal for my age.
Normal!! I feel so sad
for all the other "normal"
old gits out there.

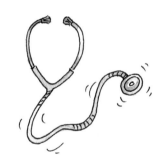

Senior moments!

For a while today
I thought I had two wives –
then I remembered
we recently had
a full length mirror
installed in the bedroom.

March 11

I had to run for the bus this morning. I must admit that I am not as fast as I used to be. I missed the first three but managed to catch the one after that.

October 24

I am always finding new ways of avoiding
senior moments. I keep a pair of spectacles
in every room of the house and my address written
on my door key – If I could only remember
which house is mine I could get a pair of spectacles
and then be able to read the address
on my keyring.

From time to time my wife and I
play an amusing little game.
We see which one of us can remember
the most of our grandchildren's names.

Senior moments!

I'm really rather dismayed for it seems
that nowadays most people look much older
than their actual age. I first noticed it
when I joined an over-fifties dating site –
I have met a number of people now
and I swear each one looks twenty
years older than stated on their profile.

March 13

I hate computer passwords.
I forget them immediately
after creating them!
Now I have a solution,
I use the same password
for all my accounts,
one that I can always remember.
Now when asked
for my password
I confidently enter
"ICANNOTREMEMBER".

October 22

Dear Diary:

This morning when I woke I couldn't find
my dentures. They were not in the glass
beside the bed. I searched the bedroom, the
bathroom, the kitchen and everywhere else.
I was really beginning to panic
when it suddenly occurred to me...
I have all my own teeth!

Senior moments!

Frank and Audrey were at the funeral of Frank's friend, Danny. At the graveside Frank stood silently with tears in his eyes.

"I know you're thinking that now it's Danny's turn but soon it will be yours."

"Actually no." replied Frank, "I was just trying to remember if Danny ever gave me back that money he owed me."

October 21

Today I made three new friends.
Well to be more precise
I suddenly remembered
the names of three friends
I had completely
forgotten about!

March 15

Dear Diary:

I have never felt so embarrassed
in all of my life. I thought the doctor
said. "Will you marry me?"
It turned out she actually said,
"I am going to give you some pills
for your gout."
I wish that I hadn't been quite
so enthusiastic...

Senior moments!

I fell down the stairs
in the house again today.
It won't happen again –
at the top of the stairs
I have put up a huge sign,
"Warning:
You are not on
the ground floor."

Dear Diary:

I had to phone the police
this morning to report that my
television and sofa had been stolen.
They were very helpful this time,
when they pointed out
that I was standing in the bathroom
not the lounge.

October 19

After a whirlwind romance, eighty year old Edward
and seventy year old Yanti got married.
Friends thought it was all too quick. However, when asked
why they had rushed into marriage Yanti explained,
"We had to marry urgently – that way we may have time
to fit in a painful breakup
and a messy divorce before we die."

March 17

My memory is awful,
last week I forgot to forget
to go to my brother's
birthday party -
I had a miserable time!

Five Steps to Longevity:

* Don't drink.

* Eat healthily.

* Don't smoke.

* Exercise frequently.

* *Be totally miserable!*

Dear Diary:
I had to be rushed
to hospital today...
but at least I now
know where that skylight
window goes.

I'm seventy-two
and my mother still refers to me
as "The Baby".

You know a night out with the lads
has reached a low ebb when they start bragging
about how many pills they have to take each day.
That signals that it's time to head home...
to take all your medicines.

I was most upset when my daughter spoiled
the movie we were watching by giving away the ending.
It really didn't help when she tried to trivialise
her misdemeanour by pointing out that
I'd already watched that movie
more than twenty times in the last year.

March 20

My husband and I
have been going to
the same holiday resort
every year for the past
thirty years. It's not that we
particularly like the place –
we are just less likely
to get lost there.

October 15

Oldies' Maxim on Memory:
Old memories never die
they just slowly fade away.

March 21

Senior moments!

I can tell you about every great movie,
the words of all the hit songs,
but I haven't a clue what I had for breakfast.

October 14

Last night my husband told me to stop
acting like a six year old.
I was so angry I threw my teddy
at him then lay down on the carpet
and had a good old tantrum.

March 22

I can still do
twenty push-ups in
the morning. Though,
to be fair, I lie on my back
and push the air
up toward the ceiling.

Today I made a very long list
of all the things that are bad
about being old.
Tomorrow I will make
another attempt at trying
to think of any good things.

The salesman was flabbergasted when I asked
that my new car be painted bright pink
with purple polka dots.
But, hey, he's not the one who's going to be
searching for it in the supermarket car park.

Senior moments!

I was delighted at managing
to successfully park the car
in our garage without denting it.
I immediately rushed
into the house
to tell my husband.
It came as a bit of a shock
when he told me that
we no longer have a car.

March 24

Now that I am retired
I am surprised to discover
that I have very little
spare time.
I think I spend half the day
losing things and
the other half
trying to find them again.

"Shall I throw out this cake,"
asked Sandra,
"it's ten years past its use-by date."
"Don't do that," replied Ian,
"I've been keeping it for
a special occasion."
"What occasion?" asked Sandra.
"I can't remember," said Ian gloomily,
"that's why it's ten years past its use-by date."

March 25

I could never, ever forget
my wife's birthday...
not with all the emails,
text messages and the
dozens of reminders
she pins up all
around the house.

October 10

Senior moments!

It's sad –
senior discounts
only ever seem to apply
to things that no
self-respecting oldie
would ever want
to do or buy.

Senior moments!

Every morning I exercise.
Up and down, up and down —
at the very least twenty times.
Then I do the same routine
with my other fingers.

Today I either
got chased across Mexico City
by sinister gangsters
or I watched a very
convincing movie.

I have a terrible sense of direction.
Recently I came out of a shop in the local mall
and turned right instead of left.
It wasn't until I reached the beach after twelve miles
that it occurred to me that there was nowhere
in the mall that has seagulls and sand.

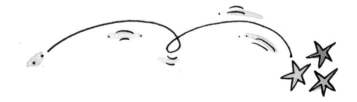

Doctors are too young.
Police Officers are too young.
Fire Fighters are too young.
Nurses are too young.
Nowadays everyone
is far too young – except me.

Everything irritates me.
Everything annoys me.
Everything frustrates me.
It would appear
that I have turned into
a Grumpy Old Man.

Last night a lady came
to my house collecting
money for a charity
that helps the aged.
I gave her some money –
she gave it
straight back to me.

It's William's sixty-fifth birthday and his best friend James is organising a surprise birthday party. James has arranged for a magician to make a birthday cake appear out of a hat. The magician needs to know one final detail – how to recognise the birthday boy.

"That's easy," said James, "he'll be the one sitting in the corner crying."

October 6

Dear Diary:
I have no idea
what I did today.
Sorry.

Every time a parcel arrives in the post I get ever so excited. Opening parcels always makes me feel as if it's my birthday. I love the anticipation of opening them, wondering what can be inside – it works every time even though it's something I ordered just days before.

October 5

Life:
by the time you reach
the age of seventy
all your older siblings
will look much
younger than you.

Senior moments!

At my time of life
I have no need for days,
weeks or months.
If asked my age
I do my very best to guess
to the nearest decade.

October 4

I completed a 10 kilometre race today.
I hadn't intending doing it –
I was just in the village and all these people
began running so I started running too –
I thought there must be a fire.

Senior moments!

I have started playing football and have joined
an over sixties team. I thought I played well
in my first game as I scored four goals.
However, the team captain was not pleased.
He told me to do exactly the same next week
but to score against the opposition.

October 3

Senior moments!

I don't trust the GPS
in my car.
Last time I used it
I went round a square
twenty-four times
before I could find
the fourth exit.

Senior moments!

Angela,
"What do you miss most about
being young?"
Fiona,
"Looking forward
to retirement."

I was at the science museum
today and a young lad
asked me if there were dinosaurs
when I was a little boy.
It made me worried
because I couldn't remember
whether or not there were.

April 3

Senior moments!

I have found that
the moment I work out
how to use a piece
of technology
all its functions will be
automatically updated.

October 1

I remember days
from fifty years ago
like they were yesterday
and yesterday as if
it were fifty years ago.

Senior moments!

"How would you feel if you were told you only had six months to live?" Karen asked her friend. "That depends," replied Gillian pensively, "if the six months were in 2082 I'd be quite happy."

September 30

Senior moments!

Today I had a long conversation in the supermarket with a very nice lady. All the time I was desperately struggling to remember her name and worrying whether I should be asking how her children are doing. She couldn't remember my children either. But then after twenty minutes we both suddenly realized that we had never met each other before.

!!@*!@*?!*@*

When I was young I would often
stay out all night partying and get to bed
at 10am. I still go to bed at 10am but now
that's for my morning nap.

I have always considered myself to be young in spirit but maybe I'm going to have to rethink that.

Apparently as you get older you get wiser.
By that measure I must have
an IQ of over 200. It's just a pity
the Wi-Fi connection to the Hard-Drive of my brain
seems to have been disconnected.

I don't go in for this healthy eating fad.
No carrots, kale or nuts for me.
I like a good fry-up in the morning,
lots of cakes in the afternoon.
When I lie pampered in hospital
I want you to know
that I've worked hard to be here.

I can remember
faces but never names...
Sometimes it's neither.

I may be eighty-eight but I've still got what it takes to keep the ladies interested – a twenty seat home cinema in my basement.

When you're my age,
if it's not sore now it will be sore later.

The police arrived at the door,
unhappy with the way
I'd parked my car.
Apparently you're not
allowed to park in
the middle of the road.

Brain speed relative to age.

Age 0 to 20: Faster than lightning.

Age 21 to 40: As fast as a speeding bullet.

Age 41 to 60: Similar speed as a marathon runner.

Age 61 to 70: About the speed of a clown riding a unicycle.

Age 71 plus: Would have difficulty keeping pace with a sloth on tranquilisers.

Today I joined the hashtag revolution.

#IAMNOTTOOOLDTOBECOOL

April 10

I find that it's getting harder to wobble in a straight line.

September 24

I'm ninety
and still have my own teeth –
I keep them in a wooden display box
that I had specially made.

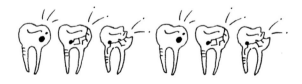

April 11

Senior moments!

I recently had to have a hearing aid fitted
as my hearing is beginning to deteriorate
– I wasn't happy with it so I made
an appointment to see the audiologist.
"Do you want me to adjust the volume
setting," she asked.
"No," I replied,
"I want you to fit an on-off switch –
my husband never stops talking."

When you reach the age of seventy,
time becomes your prisoner and your liberator.
While you become free to explore life
in ways never before possible you also become
aware that your life sentence
is rapidly decreasing.

Senior moments!

I act like a 10 year old.
I dress like a 20 year old.
I think like a 30 year old.
Oh!!! If only I looked like
a 40 year old.

Senior moments!

My wife asked the question that all men dread,
"Does my bum look big in this?"
Unfortunately I gave an honest reply.
My wife sulked for an hour then
came up with an ingenious method
so that I will never again
think her bum looks too big –
she put a paper bag over my head.

Eighty year old Dara marries Juliet.
They reach their honeymoon hotel and decide to have a nap.
Dara places his walking stick against the bedside chair,
and then his wig, spectacles, hearing aid and false teeth.
Juliet is looking perplexed and dithers.
"I'm just trying to decide
if I would be closer to you on the bed
or on the chair."

September 21

I can still do all the things
I enjoyed doing
when I was young;
sit on the couch,
watch television and
drink tea.

I complained to my wife
that the television show
I was watching was rather monotonous.
That's when she pointed out
that I had been staring
at the washing machine
for more than thirty minutes.

I'm ninety-six you know
but when I'm all dressed up
and have my wig and make-up on
I could pass for someone
of ninety!

I felt a strange mix of delight and disappointment
as I watched on television as the lottery numbers
were drawn. Delighted that, after putting on
the exact same numbers for over twenty years,
I had finally won the jackpot.
This was followed by disappointment –
that for the very first time
I had forgotten to enter.

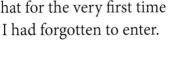

September 19

Since we retired my wife has become
obsessed with housework.
Every day she vacuums all the carpets twice
and dusts everything that doesn't move
and a few things that do.
In fact right now she is washing the windows
and French polishing the furniture...
That reminds me – I haven't painted
the bedroom doors for almost a week.

My husband's snoring
was becoming so loud
that I insisted we sleep
in separate beds.
It worked –
his bed is in
Worcester
and mine in
Birmingham.

September 18

Senior moments!

M y wife surprised me this morning by announcing
that it was our 60th wedding anniversary.
I think I annoyed her however
when I asked, "Remind me, did I marry you in the end,
or did I marry your sister?"
Well how was I to know!

Today I found
the fountain of youth –
it was switched off.

Recently I visited my doctor
for my annual check-up.
He asked me if I have any
difficulty bending over.
"Not in the slightest," I replied,
"but getting back up again
is almost impossible!"

April 18

Dear Diary:
I have just found my spectacles in the refrigerator.
Now, I wonder where I put that bottle of milk!

September 16

Why is it that I remember the words
to every single song from the 1960's
but if I'm going to the supermarket
for four things
I need to make a shopping list?

Senior moments!

For his eightieth birthday Robert had a series of flying lessons.
Soon he was allowed to fly solo for the first time but,
shortly after take-off, the plane tumbled from the sky.
Robert managed to bring it under control and landed
in a nearby field. The worried instructor rushed to the plane.
Bewildered, Robert asked
"What does the button marked 'OFF' do?"

September 15

By the time
you reach 75 years of age
you've learnt everything.
All you have to do
is to try and remember it.

Senior moments!

Last night I spent
several hours searching
for my phone.
No luck – but at least
I know where
the remote control,
kettle and microwave
disappeared to.

Senior moments!

At the home for the elderly
where I now live, a group of us
have formed a nudist club.
Well, when I say nudist club
in reality it's just that
we often forget to get dressed
before going to breakfast.

April 21

Senior moments!

I have solved my forgetfulness problem. It was simple. I just keep a pen with me at all times and write anything of importance on my hand. So today, when my wife sent me out to get the week's shopping I wrote on my left hand, "Go to the supermarket," and on my right hand, "Go back home." I bought nothing.

September 13

Senior moments!

When I turned sixty-five my wife announced that from that point on all of our vacations would be on cruise liners. Apparently at that age taking two cruises a year becomes compulsory.

I do not fear death.
I see death as a comma
rather than
a question mark.

When you have
a "Senior Moment",
you will only forget
the important things.

I have just calculated
that I have been alive
for 2,907,521,027 seconds.
Sadly I have wasted
14,211 of those seconds
doing the calculation.

Two of my good friends are soon to marry.
They are both eighty-five. They have done
this modern thing of creating a Wedding List.
Theirs is with the local pharmacist and includes
useful gifts such as sleeping tablets,
rheumatism cream and blood pressure pills.

April 24

Senior moments!

The problem with
my new-fangled
cell phone is that
I can never find
the slot to
insert my coins.

September 10

If I haven't done three
crazily impossible things
before breakfast
I know it's going to be
a drearily boring day.

I tried out those new self-service checkouts at the supermarket and got a very loud message that there was an "unexpected item in the bagging area." Really – how was I supposed to know that the little shelf was not for sitting on?

September 9

Senior moments!

!!!?/!!?!!!

I just can't get the hang of the car's SatNav.
Earlier today we were out
for a drive in the country.
It wasn't until we had driven
200 metres into the sea
that we realised that I had entered
the wrong destination code again.

Yippeeee –
I found a bowl of money.
That will make up for
the one I lost yesterday
at the very same spot!

My husband and I were having
a philosophical discussion on why we didn't
want a divorce. Sadly, top of the list,
is that we are both too old and set in our
ways to make the effort.

I have an obsession for buying fitness videos – though I must admit that the intensity of the exercises I undertake has rapidly decreased in recent years.
My latest purchase is entitled, "Gentle exercises you can do while relaxing on your sofa drinking tea."

I tried out my new telescope
this evening
but saw nothing –
tomorrow I'm going
to try using it outside.

April 28

Senior moments!

Despite his age my husband, bless him,
will still have a go at fixing anything around the house
that goes faulty.
Despite my age I'll still have a go at finding an expert
to sort out every one of his disasters.

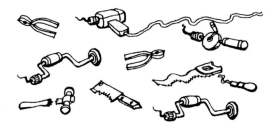

Finally I have found
a make-up
that completely hides
wrinkles –
it's two parts sand
to one part cement.

Senior moments!

At 15 you get a thrill from riding a bicycle.

At 25 you get a thrill from riding a Harley Davidson.

At 55 you get a thrill from riding a fast sports car.

At 75 you get a thrill from lying flat out on a comfy sofa.

If I could invent a machine
that could transform me
to any age of my choosing
I would set it to take me
back to the halcyon days
of my youth...
perhaps back to being
sixty or sixty-two again.

I can't sleep at night.
I often tried counting sheep
but last night one got stuck
while jumping over a style.
I lay awake for hours
trying to work out
how to set it free again.

September 4

My hearing has gone.
My eyesight has gone.
I can barely walk.
Thank goodness
I am still able to drive.

A lifetime of experience has taught me
that there is no household appliance
that can't be fixed
if you use a large enough hammer.

September 3

Good news.
I will never, ever
get lost again –
I have had a vehicle
tracking device
fitted
to my walking stick.

May 2

Old age crept up on me like a steam train hurtling off the edge of a cliff.

With a bit of a giggle Aurel tells her friend,
Richard, that he has a vitamin tablet
stuck in his left ear and a cod liver oil capsule
stuck in his right ear.
"Oh dear," replies Richard,
"that explains why my pills were
so crunchy this morning and
I'm having difficulty hearing."

May 3

I've reached that age
when they don't put
candles on my cake –
they light a bonfire
in the garden instead –
it's less dangerous.

I have started
to get cravings for
pickled onions – I hope
it's an old-age thing –
I don't want to start
a family
in my eighties!

I considered buying a wig
but instead opted to have my body hair
transplanted onto my head.
It looks very good most
of the time but whenever
I sneeze it does an impression
of a field of wheat in a hurricane.

I make no attempt to remember
my age – that would seem
so calculating. Instead I tell everyone
that I am forty-nine.
There is something beautiful about
forty-nine as an age – and I see
no reason why any lady should
ever exceed it.

May 5

I am dreadful at remembering to take back my library books. Yesterday I took back one overdue book that I hadn't even got round to reading.
I wish I hadn't taken it back – now I'm going to have to sell the car to pay the fine...
It was due back in October 1963!

August 30

The police stopped Jenny because
she was driving the wrong way
down the road. Jenny was surprised –
she hadn't realised she was driving
in the wrong direction.
"Surely you heard all the cars tooting at you?"
said the officer.
"So is that what the noise was?"
said Jenny, "I thought my tinnitus
was acting up."

A new friend visited me today.
He said he thought that my
antique furniture collection was amazing.
"Don't be so cheeky my-lad," I reprimanded,
"I bought all of these things
when they were brand new."

August 29

I do not like new things
so I always feel nervous in January.
It takes until about March
for me to resign myself
to the fact that the old year
isn't ever coming back.

"How old are you?"
asked the little boy.
"Very, very old,"
I replied.
"Fifty?"
quizzed the young lad.
"Best think
very, very, very, very old,"
I said softly.

My great granddaughter
and I have so much in common.
We both wobble as we walk
and dribble our food.

"Honey I've lost something in the kitchen," shouted Gerry. "What now?" replied Debbie. "The refrigerator," came the exasperated response.

August 27

Stairway to Heaven?
There better not be!
If the only way to get there
is by climbing a massive
flight of stairs then
I'm going to be stuck here
on Earth
for a very long time!!

Senior moments!

I can't possibly be 80! I don't think I could even count that high any more.

It is with deep regret that I am having to redefine my goals. All my life I have wanted to be an astronaut and travel to Mars but I am now eighty and NASA refuse to reply to my pleading emails requesting training. So my new ambition is go to a marathon – I vow that one day I will be there to watch all the runners finish.

"Old age gets us all..." philosophized Sarah.
"No matter whether we are rich or poor."
"Don't be silly," interrupted Lucy-Anne,
"it's so much easier for rich people like me."
"Why do you think that?" asked Sarah.
"Well, the poor need to forget things all
by themselves, whereas I have a partner
who forgets things for me."

August 25

Senior moments!

Today I rode my bicycle for an hour without going anywhere. I must remember to unchain it from that lamppost.

May 11

Old age
is like trying
to run up
a down-escalator
during an
earthquake.

August 24

Senior moments!

I can never remember what I need at the local store so I've developed a new technique. I look around for a shopping trolley that's full and take that when the shopper isn't looking. It's brilliant! I get most of the things I need and it even saves me shopping time.

May 12

Senior moments!

It's a slow progression – the more you age
the more things begin to hurt.
First it may be your knees, then your hands,
your hips will follow, soon afterwards
it's your eyes. Then, one morning,
you wake up and realize that your knees
don't hurt anymore and your hands
are less painful. That's when you really
need to start worrying.

I said to my friend,
"I seem to be losing my sense of taste,
these toffees are inedible!"
That's when she suggested
I remove the wrappers.

May 13

Red to stop. Green to go.
Red to stop. Green to go.
Red to stop. Green to go.
I really must try not to forget
that light sequence ever again.

Senior moments!

Technology is advancing too quickly
for me – I have only just mastered
changing the needle on
the gramophone and now they've
gone and put all music into tiny
little boxes that get attached
to your ears.

May 14

All those youthful years
of scrimping and scraping
to save for my retirement
and here I am,
seventy and wealthy,
and way too
knackered to enjoy it.

For most of this morning
I thought I was being followed
by a secret agent who looked
strangely familiar...
then I remembered I was out
shopping with my wife.

Today, I spent a very pleasant morning
sitting in the sun-soaked garden
eating cucumber sandwiches
and trying to remember my cat's name.

August 20

My eyesight is going.
My hearing is going,
...and I'm sure
there was something else.

May 16

Dear Diary:

My wife tells me that we had the most
incredible sex last night.
I remember
having my hot chocolate drink in bed
and then falling asleep
while reading my book.
I'm sure if I had been there while
we had incredible sex
I would have some sort of
recollection of it.

I'm a strict vegetarian... I think.

Senior moments!

A whole lifetime of dieting
and here I am at 86
overweight and unfit…
and for the very first time,
I really don't give a damn.

I love my garden shed. I go there often for a bit of sanctuary, to get away from the world. It's a real man-cave with smells of engine oil and rows of tools hanging in neat rows. Unfortunately my husband doesn't appreciate my pink curtains, frilly table cloths and cuddly soft toy collection.

May 18

I have joined a gym and now have my own personal fitness coach. I am concentrating on weight training to help improve my muscles and bones. He has started me lifting balloons and hopes that I can progress to tennis balls soon.

I asked my husband, "Will you still love me
when we are eighty?" "Just be thankful," he replied,
"if I can still remember who you are."

Apparently I used to
suffer from
athazagoraphobia –
but I've forgotten
all about that now.

August 16

The family is worried – just because I told them
I want to be buried at sky.

Today I took my grandson to the zoo.
As we walked around looking at the animals he made
comments about how fashionable I looked
in my trendy jeans. To be honest I thought he was
making fun of me – it wasn't until later
that I realised that in my haste I'd put on my old
decorating trousers – they have tears and holes
all over them. Fashion? Nonsense!

August 15

Senior moments!

Yesterday I found
a grey hair.
Yippeeee –
for years my wife
has called me "baldy".
There will be
no more of that!

May 21

Dear Diary:

Apparently it is poor etiquette
to jump the obstacles at a gymkhana
competition if you are not riding
a horse.
I won't be trying that again –
I have been banned!

I despair! I really do despair!
When I got home from the library
I discovered that my wife
had organised a surprise party
for my 80th birthday.
Surprise?
Shock of my life more like!

May 22

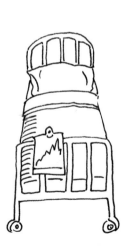

I go to the hospital
so often
they have given me
a Loyalty Card.

I am not sure whether
I now do everything in slow-motion
or if reality has suddenly
got an awful lot faster.

!!!?/!!?!!!

May 23

As I have aged I have become
the ultimate expert
on all political matters.
So much so that during news
and political programmes
on the television I have the right
to incessantly shout my views
at the screen.

August 12

Senior moments!

I can't understand the complex science
behind it but I know for a fact
that it happens – whenever
I lose something I find it
in the very last place that I look.

Every year we have
the grandchildren round to play
Treasure Hunt in our garden.
We had a pretty good haul this year;
three trowels, two pairs of secateurs
and a set of false teeth.

August 11

I saw Romeo and Juliet
today for the fifth time
this week. Wow -
that's a shocking ending -
I didn't see that coming.

May 25

Lesson One:
You have not gone deaf –
it's just the volume control
on your hearing aid.

Senior moments!

I took the dog
for a five mile walk today.
I had gone two miles before
I realised that the leash
was attached
to my granddaughter's
giant teddy.
I wondered why we were
going so slowly!

Senior moments!

I find all this new technology
stuff very baffling
and to be honest I can manage
my toaster perfectly well
without the ability
to switch it on from
the other side of the Planet!

Senior moments!

I am fed up with looking into mirrors
and seeing my wrinkly old face –
so today I took decisive action.
I printed off some wonderful photos
of my face that were taken
when I was twenty
and have stuck them on every mirror
in the house.

I don't feel old
and I don't look old
and yet it's soon my
sixtieth birthday.
Could be my fiftieth?
Maybe.

Sometimes
I find myself
standing in my
pyjamas not sure
if I am going
to bed or
getting up.

May 28

Dear Diary:

This has been a wonderful day.
I didn't get lost once. I didn't have
the embarrassment of meeting someone
whose name I couldn't remember.
I didn't buy courgettes instead of milk
at the supermarket. Yes – I have had
a great day sitting with my feet up
watching box sets on the television.

Senior Moments:
you will remember
in vivid detail
a trip to the zoo
you had when you were
five but forget
that you put food
in the pot
five minutes ago.

"Alice, for my hundredth birthday celebration
I'd like to make love to you for six hours," declared Wilson.
"Ohhhh," replied Alice, feeling rather thrilled,
"would you like me to buy a sexy nightie?"
"No thanks," said Wilson,
"but could you get me a good supply of energy pills
and a pack of super-strength Viagra tablets."

I have something so important to tell you,
I mean, sometimes in the middle of a sentence...
mmm ur mm...

I am determined to live every day
as if it were my last.
To waste no time to mediocrity.
To fill each moment with challenge,
adventure and excitement.
That is why my sink is filled
with rancid dishes –
I refuse to waste a single ray
of my sunset on boring trivia.

August 5

When you are too slow
to answer the telephone
it will be an important call –
when you manage
to reach it on time
it will be a nuisance call.

May 31

Senior moments!

"Ah, a moonlit walk along the beautiful sands of the Bahamas just like we did on our honeymoon," I said.

"Seychelles," interrupted my wife, "it was the Seychelles."

"That was every bit as romantic as forty-four years ago." I continued.

"Forty-two years ago," interjected my wife tetchily.

"Just checking," I said, in a soft voice, "your name is Elizabeth?"

Senior moments!

The internet terrifies me.
Just yesterday I was looking at
share prices on it and I accidentally
clicked on something –
I have no idea what I did
but it seemed to have caused
the stock market to crash.
By the end of the day stock prices
had plummeted by 8%.

June 1

Senior moments!

I taught my cat, Elsie, to remind me when it's her feeding time. Poor Elsie is getting as forgetful as me. She seems to be reminding me eight times a day. It's costing me a fortune!

August 3

I keep a notepad with me at all times and write
in it all the things that I must remember.
The most important thing I must remember
is emblazoned in block capitals on the front:
WRITE DOWN
THE THINGS YOU MUST REMEMBER.

June 2

Senior moments!

Yesterday I met a long lost friend –
She said I hadn't seen her for nearly two days.

August 2

Senior moments!

Today my wife drove through
a series of red lights without any
attempt at stopping.
I was getting more and more anxious
and, I must admit, a bit annoyed
at her reckless driving.
So it came as a bit of a shock
when she shouted
that I was the one who was
meant to be driving.

These days even though I use my own name
as my email password,
I will forget it every time I try to log in.

: ✳ : ✳ · ! / / · ✳ · ??? ✳ ✳ ·

August 1

Senior moments!

It was the first day of the philosophy course and eighty year old Martin sat in the front row. A young lad sat beside him and said, "I think you're amazing undertaking this difficult course. But how are you able to remember all the complex concepts and theories?"

"Actually I can't," confessed Martin, "I keep failing the exams – this is about the tenth year I've repeated the course."

June 4

It's not old age
that causes me
to be forgetful –
it's having things
to remember
that does it.

July 31

I'd give up
thirty years of my life
to be thirty years
younger.

Old Age:

When you have an emergency bag of pyjamas, slippers and toiletries always at the ready for your next hospital dash.

My wife threatened to have me replaced by a robot. No chance. Where's she going to find a robot with, a dodgy hip and the ability to completely forget everything she ever tells it?

When you are young
staying too long in a hot bath
makes your skin all wrinkly.
When you are old
staying too long
in a hot bath
makes your wrinkles
all wrinklier.

I used to do a lot of long distance hill walking.
Now my routes are very short
and have to be carefully chosen based on the frequency
and suitability of toilets.

I didn't realize when I had my heart attack
that it would be the start of a game
of one-upmanship. I have four stents
so that beats all my friends.
One tried to gain an advantage by
claiming that his two were the biggest.
However, we are now all trumped
by anyone with a pacemaker!

Having reached the ripe old age of seventy-seven
I realise that some of my ambitions are now
unrealistic and possibly unachievable.
Now, instead of wanting to become an astronaut
I have decided to try to become a Spanish dancer –
castanettes and all!

June 8

I'm still up with the fashion.
I still wear the trendy stuff
that twenty year olds wear.
And, truthfully,
I could still pass for a
twenty-something…

Senior moments!

It was coming up to their 50th wedding anniversary and Molly was keen that she and her husband, Peter, renew their wedding vows. However, Peter was not so keen. After a rather heated debate Peter demanded to know why Molly was so determined to have the ceremony. "Because," she replied hesitantly, "You're not the man I married, at least half of you has been replaced since then."

Old? If I were a cat I'd be 532!

I really don't feel
as if I'm eighty-two...
which is probably
just as well
because I think I've just
turned sixty-five.

June 10

I am terrified of sneezing. There is such a high risk of someone being knocked unconscious by one of my body parts flying off at high speed.

Senior moments!

Today I took my new glasses
back to the opticians as they are
completely useless.
They actually said they are not my glasses –
just my swimming goggles.

June 11

Senior moments!

I can remember Citizen Kane
as if I'd watched it
just a few months ago —
but actually I think
I saw it yesterday.
Or was it Wuthering Heights!

My grandson was surprised
when he saw that I had several stamps
stuck to my computer screen.
Apparently you don't need stamps
to send an email.

June 12

I had a bit of a panic today,
I thought my garden
had been invaded by
wild beasts but it was okay,
I had just wandered
into the lion enclosure
at the zoo.

The terrible truth is that
immediately after buying a replacement
you will find the item you had lost.

I wake up in the middle of the night
knowing the answer to Life, the Universe and Everything.
But I've forgotten.

July 22

Mary astounded the researchers for although
she was seventy the laboratory tests showed
she had a physical age of thirty.
They analysed everything she ate, drank
and did but couldn't find the reason
for her youthfulness. Confused, they asked
Mary's opinion. Pensively she replied,
"It's simple. I've never owned a watch so
I have no way of measuring the passage of time."

Senior moments!

I woke at 3am convinced
that I'd forgotten to put
the cat out last night.
It wasn't until I discovered
my husband shivering
on the doormat
that I remembered
we don't have a cat.

July 21

I took up Bridge to help
my memory and build
friendships. But I keep
forgetting the rules
and now no one
is speaking to me.

June 15

I was trying to add some hieroglyphics
to a text message I was sending
but was having great difficulty.
Fortunately my granddaughter
was around and could explain to me
that they are now called emojis.

The dog is acting very strangely
today, it keeps meowing.
And my wife calling,
"Here Kitty" isn't helping.

June 16

As ninety-two year old Jennifer crossed the finish line at the Edinburgh Marathon, the clock showed 3 Hours 59 minutes.
A young runner rushed up to congratulate her,
"Wow, that was amazing you finished in under four hours,"
he shouted with admiration.
"Not so amazing," gasped Jennifer, "I actually started out with last year's runners."

When you are old
the future holds
great mystery -
as does the past.

Whenever I need the answer
to a complicated issue I ask my cat.
I never get an answer
but it saves me wearing my brain out
puzzling over the problem.

"I remember our trip to Egypt
as if it was yesterday," I said to my wife.
"We've never been to Egypt,"
she replied. "Right! Well, if we haven't been,
how come I remember it so well?"
I asked. "Because you were reading
the Lonely Planet Guide yesterday
you daft old trout,"
she responded rather too gleefully.

June 18

Senior moments!

I was on one of those high speed trains recently.
Gosh they are super-fast –
I'd gone six stops before I even reached a seat.

My wife is becoming forgetful –
she keeps saying the same thing to me
over and over again. In fact there's
not a day goes by when she doesn't
turn to me and say,
"You've told me that joke before
you daft old codger."

Sometimes I feel like an actress who has forgotten her lines surrounded by people who have forgotten how to act.

I lost three good friends last week...
that's the last time I go hill walking with them –
not a map or compass between them!

I don't really need glasses.
In fact I only ever wear them when it's absolutely
necessary to see.
And then I've sat on them again.

July 15

The theory of retirement is that you work hard all your life and save all your money – then you retire and are able to do all the things you couldn't do before. But you hadn't included grandchildren in your plan. Now you spend all your time looking after screaming children and taking them on trips and all your money buying them gifts.

I rarely watch television –
in fact it's only
on the rare occasions
that the remote turns up
that I even bother
to switch it on.

I got confused
and took my golf clubs
instead of my rods
on a fishing trip.
I was so distracted
that it wasn't until
I'd caught three salmon
that I realised my mistake.

June 22

In your twenties you live
close to shops and nightclubs.
In your thirties
you move to be close to a good
school for your children.
In your seventies
you move again to be close to
your favourite hospital.

Dear Diary:

I ran a marathon today.
I must remember
to ask the organisers
of that 10 kilometre race
if they could make
the direction signs
bigger next year.

June 23

I would do anything
to be fit again –
in fact yesterday
I very nearly
considered doing
two push-ups.

I love gardening but,
with my multitude of
ailments, I can't do
nearly as much as
I used to. Now my
philosophy is,
if a weed grows
don't kill it – enjoy it.

June 24

My bedtime routine can often be disrupted by my poor memory. Sometimes I forget to floss, sometimes I forget to put on my pyjamas and recently I completely forgot to go to bed at all.

When I was ten I thought
that thirteen was old.
When I was eighteen
I thought twenty-one was old.
Now that I am the
ripe old age of ninety-five
I consider one-hundred
to be decidedly ancient.

Senior moments!

Old age is underrated,
there are many advantages
to being of
a "mature" age –
and as soon
as I can think of some
I will let you know.

July 10

I love reading
but sometimes
I get to the end of a book
and discover
it's the wrong end.

June 26

I was very upset
when the supermarket assistant
told me that she loved my beard.
I'm telling you –
that nasal hair
is getting trimmed today.

* !! * ?! *

I find that I'm now very quick to
anger. But then I quickly forget
what I'm angry about...
then I get angry that I've forgotten
what I was angry about...
and then I forget that...

June 27

When I looked out of the window this morning
I got a dreadful shock – the whole area was flooded.
Everywhere I looked, for miles and miles
all I could see was water. It was a great relief
when people told me I was on a cruise ship.

I was awestruck this morning
when I discovered
that my wife is some forty years
younger than me.
Sadly I'd just walked into
the wrong house.

June 28

Senior moments!

I went to the optician
and said,
"My eyesight is getting
really bad."
"Sure is," came the reply,
"I'm your husband."

July 7

When I was young I was always
desperately seeking love.
Now that I am old I have found it...
I love my cooker,
I love my microwave,
I love my television,
I love my computer...

Senior moments!

You don't realise you are old
until you are rushing
up a hill and a mother
with a pram, two children,
three full shopping bags
and a dog
pass you at speed.

July 6

Senior moments!

I sometimes
get that sense of déjà vu –
when I do something
for the seventh time.

June 30

On mornings
such as this
I must remember
that the world
is not upside down
– I have merely
fallen out of bed.

July 5

Senior moments!

I read that eating
a large portion of broccoli
every day helps to
improve memory.
I've decided that
having a bad memory
isn't so bad after all.

On turning seventy Graham decided
that he needed a Big Adventure
to prove he was still young.
"I am going to run across Africa,"
he announced. "Don't be daft," replied
his wife, "you often get lost going
to the local shop."
"Ahhhh," replied Graham gleefully,
"I've thought of that one –
I'm going to take a huge ball of string."

My wife teases me that I tell the same joke
every time we meet up with our friends.
Oh yeah! Well, how can that be for they find it
so hilarious every time?

July 2

I am not old, I am just ahead of my time.

I seem to have become expert
in napping. I am able to nap
on a bus, on a train, in the bath –
anywhere.
The only time
I have difficult napping
is at night – I suffer dreadfully
with insomnia.

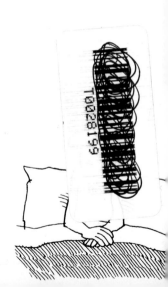